*This book was first written in English
and then translated into French by the author
so that it could be presented in a bilingual edition.*

Praise for *Dreaming My Animal Selves*

In this extraordinary volume of soul crafted poetry, words become wands to enchant and evoke our better angels.

~ Jean Houston
(Ph.D., philosopher, author of *The Wizard of Us*, *A Mythic Life*, and *Mystical Dogs*)

"Every force of nature has a purpose," writes Hélène Cardona. Dreaming My Animal Selves finds its nature not in French or English, but in the correspondences between them, the experience international, liminal, mystical and otherworldly. This is a poet who writes in a rare light.

~ David Mason
(poet laureate of Colorado and author of *The Buried Houses*, winner of the Nicholas Roerich Poetry Prize, and *The Country I Remember*, winner of the Alice Fay Di Castagnola Award)

In Dreaming My Animal Selves *the poet Hélène Cardona has become a dreamer upon two pillows of language. Taking her queue from Rilke, she has captured dreams in a diglottism of the soul, a literary isthmus of heliotrope and honeysuckle, where her singular voice endures as 'a thistle, resilient/ rooted in Mediterranean Celtic fringe.' Through poetry she reaches that gateway between the past and the way ahead. It was Gaston Bachelard who wrote that the roots of the grandeur of the world plunge back into a childhood and here, in her reflective moments, Cardona reaches back to the amethyst eyes of a Francophone childhood. Here is a poetry of exotic retreat, from the translucent face of Tibet to the Cyprus pomegranate of Athena's altar; and here, too, Aphrodite guides her to a place where she is compelled to pay for her mother's death with a literary grief extracted from dreams. It is always a risky business for a poet to self-translate; it may seem like wanting both the work of art and the readers' response — but Hélène Cardona gracefully travels across languages, in the manner of our own Michael Hartnett, Paddy Bushe, or, more lately, Fred Johnston, to arrive at a point of insight where we are all enriched.*

Dreaming My Animal Selves *is a graceful skate across a liquid language, a voyage across subliminal waves; a poetry where, as she writes in 'Parallel Keys' she reveals herself by 'fixing the omen.'*

~ Thomas McCarthy
(winner of the Patrick Kavanagh Poetry Award, author of *The Last Geraldine Officer*, *Merchant Prince*, and *Mr Dineen's Careful Parade: New and Selected Poems*)

Her multinational upbringing has blessed Hélène Cardona with, as Joseph Campbell would say, "a vision transcending the scope of normal human destiny, and amounting to a glimpse of the essential nature of the cosmos." In Dreaming My Animal Selves, Hélène presents her cosmic vision through mythic identifications with animal spirits and animal morphologies.

~ RUSTIN LARSON, *The Iowa Source*

Cardona's imagistic dream poems are timeless artifacts, little 'songs of innocence' from a primordial / universal age. Cardona's Dreaming My Animal Selves is not only a poet's spiritual awakening, but a sacred journey whereby each individual poem (or song) serves as a marker within the larger map of her inner geography, a map which, in turn, guides her through and breathes her back into her physical world with a renewed vigor.

~ MARC VINCENZ, *The Lit Pub*

Hélène Cardona's poetry is full of wonder and, like all good poetry, is not bound by conventional rules of language or logic, but free as in dreams. Reading Hélène, one feels the fetters of mundane living loosening. Like Lorca, she traces oneiric patterns and pursues elusive sleep 'in the hope to heal mishaps / the last chance to anchor my boat'.

~ JAMES LAWLESS
(author of *Clearing The Tangled Wood: Poetry as a Way of Seeing the World*)

An exploration of spirit rather than body, Dreaming My Animal Selves thrums across an everyday wilderness that transcends time, geography, history, and the physical self.
  Through "beings disguised" Cardona explores the more ethereal qualities of existence – of what's between the enigma of life, death, wake, and sleep. Dreaming My Animal Selves takes readers to some sort of limbo where reality and fantasy combine to create a brief yet precise overlap of clarity. Dreaming My Animal Selves ultimately boils down to a yearning for harmony and peace in a place of shape-shifting duality. The poems are rich in myth, imagination, biology, art, language, and literature.

~ KARLI CUDE, *Typographical Era*

MORE PRAISE FOR *Dreaming My Animal Selves* on page 78

HÉLÈNE CARDONA

Dreaming My Animal Selves

Le Songe de mes Âmes Animales

A BILINGUAL COLLECTION

salmonpoetry

First Published in 2013 by
Salmon Poetry
Cliffs of Moher, County Clare, Ireland
Reprinted by Salmon Poetry in 2014
Website: www.salmonpoetry.com
Email: info@salmonpoetry.com

ISBN 978-1-908836-39-7

COVER ARTWORK: Created for *Dreaming My Animal Selves*
by Jackie Morris. www.jackiemorris.co.uk

COVER DESIGN & TYPESETTING: *Siobhán Hutson*

Printed in Ireland by Sprint Print

Acknowledgements

I am deeply thankful to Thomas McCarthy, Brian Turner, Willis Barnstone, David Mason, Jean Houston and Yves Lambrecht for their inspiration and support.

Gracious thanks to Jessie Lendennie and Siobhán Hutson at Salmon Poetry for delivering this book into the world.

My endless gratitude to my angel John Fitzgerald for all the magic.

"From the Heart With Grace" first appeared in *THRUSH Poetry Journal* and was nominated for best of the net 2012 and for the 2012 Pushcart Prize.

"Parallel Keys" first appeared as Editor's Choice in *The Enchanting Verses Literary Review*.

"Notes from Last Night", "Cornucopia", "The Sexiest Flower", "Notes d'hier soir" and "La fleur la plus séduisante" first appeared in *Recours au poème*.

"Dancing the Dream", "Illumination", "Lunar Standstill", "Heliotropic", "Transparencies of Thought", "Pathway to Gifts," "Diapositives de pensées", "Danse le rêve" and "Arrêt lunaire" first appeared in *Levure Littéraire,* Issue 6.

"Inquistive Life" first appeared in *Pirene's Fountain.*

"Avalon" first appeared in *Barnwood Mag.*

"Peregrine Pantoum" first appeared in *Barnwood Mag* and in *The Blue Max Review.*

"Dreamer" first appeared in *The American Center for Artists* and in *Mediterranean Poetry.*

"Shaman in Residence" first appeared in *Mythic Passages.*

"The Magician" first appeared in *The Passionate Transitory* and in the Anthology *For Rhino in a Shrinking World.*

"Quiescent Infinite" first appeared in *The Lascaux Review* and in *Radical Magazine.*

"In Dreams Like Rain" first appeared in *Spillway.*

"Breeze Rider" first appeared in *Saint Julian Press.*

"Isle of the Immortals", "Pathway to Gifts" and "The Magician" first appeared in the Anthology *For Rhino in a Shrinking World.*

"A Mind Like the Sky", "Night Messenger" and "Dreams Like Water" first appeared in the January 2013 Edition of *THRUSH Poetry Journal.*

Dreaming My Animal Selves was a Finalist for the Jacar Press Julie Suk Award for a Poetry Book Published by an Independent Press in 2013 and a finalist for the 2014 Readers' Favorite Book Award.

For John,
my constant companion,
with all my love.
Some search their whole lives for that elusive other
who is simply the perfect mirror.
We are beyond fortunate we found each other.

In memory of my mother Kitty,
for her love and light,
In gratitude to my father José Manuel,
the poet from Ibiza, el cisne vallisoletano,
To my brother Rodrigo, aunt Opie and grandmother Mami,
We are a family of swans.

Table des Matières

Contents

Foreword

HÉLÈNE CARDONA'S *Dreaming My Animal Selves/ Le Songe de mes Âmes Animales*, is an intriguingly surreal journey through myth, legend, fantasy, and more—all guided by a shape-shifting narrator searching far and wide for cosmic unity within the discontinuous landscape of dream and the dreamy, fragmented quality of the everyday world. The dual-language text works to heighten the narrator's shifting perceptions, symbol by symbol, vision by vision. Within the cornucopia of this collection, the narrator declares—"I travel corridors of mind…" where "…the heart/ [is] a secret tower I inhabit" and "I cut loose/ the end of sorrow." In a very real sense, *Dreaming My Animal Selves* is a book centered in joy, rooted firmly in the wild landscape of the imagination.

> ~ BRIAN TURNER
> winner of the Beatrice Hawley Award,
> author of *Here, Bullet* and *Phantom Noise*

PROLOGUE

So I am sometimes like a tree
rustling over a grave site
and making real the dream
of the one its living roots
embrace:

a dream once lost
among sorrows and songs.

~ RAINER MARIA RILKE

Des songes d'eau

Je trace les motifs des songes
au travers d'êtres déguisés
libérés en particules évanouies
révélant des éclats de moi-même.
Dans l'espoir de guérir mes naufrages,
je pourchasse un sommeil en cavale,
ultime refuge où ancrer mon vaisseau.

Dreams Like Water

I trace patterns in dreams
through beings disguised
undone like particles broken apart
revealing pieces of me.
I pursue elusive sleep
in the hope to heal mishaps
the last chance to anchor my boat.

I

If the doors of perception were cleansed,
everything would appear to man as it is, infinite.

~ WILLIAM BLAKE

I think it was from the animals
that St. Francis learned
it is possible to cast yourself
on the earth's good mercy and live.

~ JANE HIRSHFIELD

Du cœur avec grâce

Le Vent rêvant d'être dégusté
m'offre trois coupes regorgeant
d'éternité, vision éclatante.
L'opportune rencontre réenchante la désolation
de l'absolu, bouscule le calme glacial,
engendre un jeu d'esprit, glückliche Reise,
propulse les fervents parfums
de l'héliotrope, de la jacinthe et du chèvrefeuille.
L'hibiscus persifleur me fait chavirer vers les climats
ensoleillés, me rappelle que je demeure chardon,
enracinée et cousue à la frange celte et méditerranéenne.

Te rappelles-tu une langue plus ancienne
que le temps, lorsqu'un frisson parcourant l'épine
dorsale de ma mère valait plus que mille mots
et la mélancolie du regard de mon père,
reflétant le Lac Léman, était indéchiffrable?
Là, à mon insu, dans un monde
peuplé de cygnes,
je nage à mon tour en cercles concentriques
afin d'entendre l'écho de mon âme
et de découvrir qu'au cœur même du songe
réside la guérison de la terre. Nous explorons
dans le songe l'espace où tout est pardonné.
Au sein du songe est créé le divin.

Alors l'Unité divine soupire ex-voto,
je suis centaure par tout autre nom,
je suis griffon par tout autre nom,
je suis sirène par tout autre nom,
ma raison d'être chimérique, caméléon,
excavée des naufrages tel un talisman,
resplendissante fresque catapultée
au-delà de fantasques frontières métaphoriques.

From the Heart with Grace

Wind, who yearns to be savored, offers
me three cups overflowing
with eternity, daemon of insight.
The opportune encounter enraptures quintessential
distress, ruffles estranged quietude,
kindles a jeu d'esprit, glückliche Reise,
propels the fervent fragrance
of heliotrope, hyacinth and honeysuckle.
The tremulous hibiscus taunts me to warm climates,
reminds me I remain a thistle, resilient,
rooted in Mediterranean Celtic fringe.

Do you remember a language older
than time, when a shiver down my mother's
spine was worth a thousand words
and the melancholy in my father's eyes,
reflecting Lake Geneva, was indecipherable?
There unbeknownst to me
in a world inhabited by swans,
I too swim in concentric circles
to find the resonance of my core
and discover that in dreaming
lies the healing of earth. In dreaming
we travel to a place where all is forgiven.
In dreaming is the Divine created.

And the great Oneness whispers ex-voto,
I am centaur by any other name,
I am griffin by any other name,
I am mermaid by any other name,
my raison d'être insubstantial, chameleon,
excavated like a talisman from wreckage,
resplendent fresco catapulted
beyond whimsical metamorphic frontiers.

Pantoum pèlerin

Commence par un rêve,
Montagnes couronnées de neige et rivières gorgées de saumons.
Rayons verts ouvrent un passage au cœur de l'hiver,
Dansant à l'orée du lac.

Montagnes couronnées de neige et rivières gorgées de saumons
retentissent de rires et sonates de lilas
dansant à l'orée du lac.
Des contes de fée invitant à des jours sans fin

retentissent de rires et sonates de lilas,
ébauches exquises de ma grand-mère.
Des contes de fée invitant à des jours sans fin,
sagesse et mélancolie préparent des feux,

ébauches exquises de ma grand-mère,
polies par des elfes. Je dors avec ferveur.
Sagesse et mélancolie préparent des feux,
myriade de livres et maisons émouvantes

polies par des elfes. Je dors avec ferveur
sur routes glissantes, chemins verglacés.
Myriade de livres, maisons émouvantes
et forêts envoûtées dévoilent trésors et charades d'enfants.

Routes glissantes, chemins verglacés
captivent les méandres de l'esprit.
Forêts envoûtées dévoilent trésors et charades d'enfants,
exiles et voyages, forcés et choisis.

Captivant les méandres de l'esprit,
le pays des dieux retentit de récits et tortures,
exiles et voyages, forcés et choisis.
Sirènes et flûtes enchantées embrasées,

le pays des dieux retentit de récits et tortures.
Rayons verts ouvrent un passage au cœur de l'hiver,
sirènes et flûtes enchantées embrasées.
Commence par un rêve.

Peregrine Pantoum

Begin with a dream,
snowcapped mountains and rivers of salmon.
Green rays cleave the heart of winter
dancing at the edge of the lake.

Snowcapped mountains and rivers of salmon
echo laughter and lilac sonatas
dancing at the edge of the lake.
Fairy tales beckoning days on end

echo laughter and lilac sonatas,
my grandmother's exquisite designs.
Fairy tales beckoning days on end,
wisdom and melancholy build fires,

my grandmother's exquisite designs
engineered by elves. I sleep with fervor.
Wisdom and melancholy build fires,
myriad books and soulful dwellings

engineered by elves. I sleep with fervor
on slippery roads, frozen paths.
Myriad books, soulful dwellings,
enchanted forests ripen with children's riddles.

Slippery roads, frozen paths
drive mazes of mind.
Enchanted forests ripen with children's riddles,
exiles and travels, forced and chosen.

Driving mazes of mind,
tales of torture ring from the land of gods,
exiles and travels, forced and chosen.
Sirens and magic flutes ablaze,

Tales of torture ring from the land of gods.
Green rays cleave the heart of winter,
Sirens and magic flutes ablaze.
Begin with a dream.

Curiosité de vie

Et bien, j'ai parfois cru à au moins six choses
impossibles avant le petit-déjeuner.

~ LEWIS CARROLL

Mon monde féerique
temple submergé, prodigue
où parmi orages et arcs-en-ciel
tout s'oublie
l'océan annonce
Lorsque l'onde colossale surgit
l'éléphant montera
sur la girafe et tu sauras
respirer dans le creux des flots.
Et cela se produit à l'équinoxe vernal
même si c'est difficile à croire.

Inquisitive Life

Why, sometimes I've believed as many as six impossible things before breakfast.

~ LEWIS CARROLL

My elfin world
lavish, submerged temple
where amid storms and rainbows
all is forgotten
the ocean heralds
When the colossal wave arises,
the elephant will go on top
of the giraffe, and you will know
to breathe inside the hollow water.
And it happens at the Vernal Equinox
even if it's hard to believe.

Émissaire nocturne

Je m'éveille. Dans un pré
galonné d'herbes sauvages et de fleurs
des notes s'échappent d'une harpe.
Un pingouin court.
Je le talonne à la rivière.
Il se couche sur une feuille,
se laisse emporter par le courant
et dit, *ce torrent est ta vie,*
au lieu de l'observer du pré
laisse son rythme t'envahir.
Guidée par une cornemuse
j'atteins le portail
entre le passé et les flots.
Comme le pingouin, je me couche sur une feuille,
me laisse emporter par la rivière
sachant que j'ai pénétré un autre monde.

Night Messenger

I wake. In a meadow
braided with wild grasses and flowers
notes of music drift from a harp.
A penguin is running.
I follow to the river.
He lays on a leaf,
lets the current carry him
and says, *this stream is your life,*
instead of watching from the meadow,
flow with its rhythm.
Guided by Scottish pipes
I reach the gate
between my past and the waterway.
Like the penguin, I lay on a leaf,
let the river transport me
knowing I've entered another world.

Corne d'abondance

Univers magnifique créé par une force féminine
subtile, riche terre,
Éden, oiseaux mythologiques
et arbres fleurissants en apothéose.

Je parcours les corridors de l'esprit,
synapses chaotiques, amnésie frénétique,
élans captivants, paradis diffus,
pénètre temples cristallins par portails de marbre.

Le rire de Poséidon résonne : *salue*
le dragon aquatique. Avec des yeux
améthyste observe un soupçon de magie,
crocodiles souriants se transformant en tortues,

mon nom pyramide, amulette antique,
le cœur une tour secrète que j'habite.
À travers la toile que j'ai tissée je libère
la fin du chagrin. Je reste ici pour de bon.

Cornucopia

Subtle feminine power creates a magnificent
universe, rich soil,
Edenic mythological birds
and trees blooming in apotheosis.

I travel corridors of mind, synapses
of chaos, frenetic amnesia, beguiling
impulses, diffusion of heaven, past marble
portals to crystalline temples.

Poseidon's laughter resonates: *Hail
the water dragon.* With amethyst eyes
witness dashes of magic. Smiling
crocodiles turn to tortoises, my name

pyramid, antique amulet, the heart
a secret tower I inhabit. Across
the web I've woven I cut loose
the end of sorrow. I'm here to stay.

Le chemin aux dons

lorsque mon âme s'est retournée,
percevant l'autre côté du tout...

~ H.D.

Des soupirs m'éveillent.
Je rentre chez moi
à la queue d'une procession de cygnes
sur une île au cœur de Paris.
Sur les falaises où les animaux sauvages
viennent se déployer,
je siffle cette chanson,
regarde l'autre côté du monde
comme un jeu de cartes étalé
dont tu scrutes le dessous et que tu retournes
pour en voir la face cachée.
Le songe éveille les royaumes oubliés de la création.
Je pense que c'est cela le temps.

Pathway to Gifts

when my soul turned round,
perceiving the other-side of everything…

~ H.D.

Whispers wake me.
I return home
behind a procession of swans
to an island in the heart of Paris.
On the cliffs where the wild ones come
to show themselves,
I sing this whistling song,
look at the other side of the world
as if a deck of cards spread out
to peek under and flip over
for a glimpse at the hidden side.
The dream opens forgotten realms of creation.
I think that's what time is.

Notes d'hier soir

pour John, en souvenir de son père

On peut distinguer Van Gogh de Chagall,
cet état d'intervalle
où même les objets semblent vivants,
qui traite de lumière et pureté.
À cause de toute cette lumière je suis presque aveugle.
Peu importe le fantôme que tu vois
du moment que tu en vois un.
Deux pénombres liées à travers un visage,
la chaleur avance, le froid se retire.
J'en fais juste l'expérience.
Parle de foi à laquelle je ne crois,
l'expérience est cellulaire.
Dans notre état normal nous ne pouvons percevoir,
c'est pourquoi je pense que les morts savent.
Je n'avais jamais auparavant vu telle beauté,
tout est lié à la lumière.
Chaque fantôme preuve de l'après vie,
n'importe quel fantôme.

Notes From Last Night

to John, in memory of his father

One can distinguish Van Gogh from Chagall,
that state of in-betweenness
where even objects seem alive,
to do with light and looking pure.
Because of all this light, I'm partially blind.
It doesn't matter whose ghost you see
as long as you see one.
Two darknesses together across the shape
of face, warmth comes forward, cool retreats.
I just experience.
Talk about faith I don't believe,
experience is cellular.
In our normal state we're not able to perceive,
that's why I think the dead know.
I had never seen before the beauty
of it, everything has to do with light.
Every ghost proof of the afterlife,
any ghost.

II

Trust the dreams, for in them is hidden the gate to eternity.

~ KAHLIL GIBRAN

Danse le rêve

C'est une histoire d'envol,
histoire de racines,
histoire de grâce.
Je suis l'enfant vagabonde.
Chaque voyage connaît une destination secrète.
Je trouverai mon chemin sans carte
grâce au souvenir gravé dans l'étreinte de ma mère
ces nuits orageuses au pied des Alpes.
Je me retrouverai dans le cœur
d'une rose. Je regagnerai mon âme,
ancrée, centrée
où la psyché repose,
la présence du mystère si lumineuse
que son essence me comble.
Je parcours le labyrinthe,
laisse échapper les désirs emprisonnés.
J'arrache la vigne entrelacée autour du cordon
ombilical, libère les lettres de mon nom.
Elles émergent sur l'océan,
réclamées par le faucon.
Je danse le rêve
au bord d'arides royaumes ravagés.
Des ponces volcaniques et purs argiles
je récolte les délicieuses floraisons d'amour,
douce et savoureuse ambroisie de la terre.

Dancing the Dream

This is a story of flight,
a story of roots,
a story of grace.
I am the wandering child.
Every journey knows a secret destination.
I'll find my way without a map, rely
on memory embedded in my mother's embrace
on stormy nights at the foot of the Alps.
I'll find home in the heart
of a rose, retrieve my soul,
anchored in the still point
where psyche rests,
the presence of mystery so luminous
I'm infused with its essence.
I walk the labyrinth, let
go of confined desires.
I rip the vine intertwined around
the umbilical, liberate the letters of
my name. They soar above the ocean
for the falcon to reclaim.
I'm dancing the dream
on the brink of barren ravaged realms.
From volcanic pumice and pure clay
I reap scrumptious blossoms of love,
earth's sweet and savory ambrosia.

L'île des Immortels

Une lumière phosphorescente baigne
le matin. Des biches traversent la route,
m'invitent à flâner parmi les bouleaux.
Un lièvre ailé m'offre
une tortue aux marques anciennes.
Sollicitée par d'espiègles esprits,
j'ouvre un passage dans l'ampleur de la brume,
découvre bruyère, trèfles, genêt
et bourse-à-pasteur.

Le visage translucide d'un moine tibétain
disparaît dans la rosée, reflète
la face cachée de la lune.
À travers l'éclat j'observe
la danse mélodieuse de l'enchanteur
rêveur, héron lustré statuesque.
Il descend en vrille
dans le tunnel, d'un flou d'ailes
me souffle, *il peut faire du vent, accroche-toi.*
Tu apprends à vivre dans deux mondes à la fois.
Tu trouveras tout dans le noyau terrestre.
Les animaux sont nos alliés.
Tout est apparenté, une seule conscience.

L'ultime dessein est de révérer l'univers.
L'ultime dessein est d'aimer la vie.
L'ultime dessein est de s'harmoniser.
Tout comme les graines réclament les ténèbres
pour germer, j'hiberne et émerge en lumière
condensée, cultive un lien avec l'avenir.
La grenouille en moi pond un œuf
dont le pélican pure joie naît.

Guidé par le héron, notre navire
dans les nuages atteint l'île
des Immortels, l'âme resplendissante.
Je suis gardienne de l'espace, jumelle
en moi-même, me fond
avec la force vitale, alchimiste
épousant les lois supérieures.

Isle of the Immortals

Phosphorescent light bathes morning.
Deer cross the road, entice
me to meander through birches.
A winged hare offers
a turtle with ancient markings.
Solicited by playful spirits
I part the swelling mist,
chance upon heathrush, clover, broom
and shepherd's purse.

Translucent face of Tibetan monk
vanishes above the dew, reflects
the hidden side of moon.
Through the glow I witness
the melodious dance of the wistful
wizard, statuesque sleek crane.
He spirals down the water
tunnel, wings a blur, whispers,
it can be windy, hang on to me.
You're learning to live in two worlds at once.
You'll find everything at the core of the earth.
Animals are allies.
All is kin, one consciousness.

The ultimate aim is reverence for the universe.
The ultimate aim is love for life.
The ultimate aim is harmony within oneself.
The way seeds need darkness to germinate
I hibernate and emerge into condensed light,
cultivate a relationship with the future.
The frog part of me lays an egg
from which the pelican sheer joy is born.

Under the crane's guidance, our boat
in the clouds reaches the Isle
of the Immortals, the soul resplendent.
I am the space holder, twin
inside myself, blend
with the life giver, trickster
bound by higher laws.

Avalon

Tu ne m'aurais pas appelé
sans que je t'appelle.

C.S. Lewis, Aslan à Jill dans *La Chaise argentée*

Alors comment ça va au paradis?
La vue est jolie
avec des fées dans le jardin.
Une rose porte
ces vers de Ronsard—
Je vous envoie un bouquet que ma main
Vient de trier de ces fleurs épanouies.
De nouvelles branches poussent
au noyer de l'enfance.
Anna Akhmatova libère
toute l'eau emprisonnée en moi
et je grandis encore.
De la question naît une conscience
elliptique unissant passé et présent
de sorte que mes mots, *Souviens-toi*
que je t'aime, fleurissent.

Avalon

You would not have called to me unless
I had been calling to you.

C.S. LEWIS, Aslan to Jill in *The Silver Chair*

So how are things in heaven?
The view is nice
with fairies in the garden.
A rose bears
lines from the Ronsard poem –
Je vous envoie un bouquet que ma main
Vient de trier de ces fleurs épanouies.
The walnut tree of childhood
grows new branches.
Anna Akhmatova unleashes
all the water locked inside me
and I expand again.
The question creates an elliptic
consciousness, bridges past and present
till my words, *Remember*
I love you, blossom.

"I send you a wreath of blossoms
And woven flowers by my hand gathered"

En songes de pluie

Ma mère me rend visite
en songes de pluie.
Un oiseau sous la douche
prend les messages :
Traque un monde plus profond.
J'entends la voix de Blake, *traverse*
la forêt, et celle de Yeats, *reflète la lumière.*
Dans cette mare je deviens poisson.

Ma physionomie aux multiples reflets
s'ouvre comme un éventail.
Un tableau de visages bouddhistes,
je ne me reconnais pas.

Je suis la graine, semence
radiance chromatique
fleur de cerisier en cœur
déployée au vent,
danse féerique
mémoire poétique
vivante.

In Dreams Like Rain

In dreams like rain
my mother visits.
A bird in the shower
takes messages:
Stalk a deeper world.
I hear Blake's voice, *walk through
the forest*, and Yeats, *reflect the light.*
In this pool I turn into fish.

My multi facial appearance
springs open like a fan.
An array of Buddhist visages,
I don't recognize myself.

I'm the seed, kernel
chromatic radiance
cherry blossom of a heart
extended into wind
fairy dance
poetic memory
alive.

Illumination

Émergeant d'un gel profond, pieds
palmés effleurant la surface
de l'eau, ma mère imagina
ma création,
un poulain envolé à sa fenêtre.
La douleur fend la peau,
nous invite à pénétrer,
ancêtre désormais bienvenu chez moi.
Au crépuscule les mouettes prennent leur envol.
Illuminée de l'intérieur,
une arbore une lumière translucide
qui l'encercle, l'élève
et révèle, *tout est arrangé,*
c'est si facile de l'autre côté.

Illumination

Risen out of deep freeze, webbed
feet skimming across
the water, my mother imagined
I came into being,
colt flown through her window.
Pain cleaves the skin,
allows us to penetrate,
ancestor now welcome in my body.
At sunset seagulls take flight.
Illuminated from within
one carries translucent light
that shoots around her, lifts her up,
reveals, *everything is taken care of,*
it's so easy on the other side.

Chaman à demeure

À mi-chemin de son voyage
    elle se retrouve dans la baleine,
confinée à examiner sa condition,
    ce qui l'a menée aussi loin,
    ce qui se cache derrière le fanon,
    quel passage suivre.
Des souvenirs à la lisière de l'iode –
    une fille sur une balançoire
    l'étreinte bleu profond des amants
    des chevaux pêchant le poisson –
propulsent l'océan à la recracher sur le rivage,
    souffrance endiamantée, arme et joyau,
    verre de mer léché par le soleil.
Comme la terre l'accueille,
    elle pénètre ce lieu sacré
    nommé hiver, épiphanie insaisissable.
Avec un visage différent, langage liquide,
    elle s'écoule dans le sable en quête de trésors.

Shaman in Residence

Halfway through the journey
    she finds herself inside the whale,
confined to mull her condition over,
    what led this far,
    what lies behind the baleen,
    what passageway to heed.
Memories transpire on the edge of iodine –
    girl on a swing
    deep blueness of lovers' embrace
    horses catching fish –
till ocean expels her on the shore,
    diamond pain, weapon and jewel,
    sea glass licked by the sun.
The way land greets her,
    she enters this sacred
    place called winter, elusive epiphany.
With a different face, liquid language,
    she seeps into sand in search of treasures.

Cavalière de la brise

Chaque force de la nature a sa raison d'être.
     Je maintiens l'équilibre de la planète.
Quand on sent que je suis là
          on est élevé.

À voyager par vent
          on atteint des endroits autrement impossibles,
               question de qualité.

Le but est de laisser l'esprit
          couler au lieu de stagner,
               laisse-le gronder tel un fleuve.

Si on essaie d'en garder un morceau,
          trophée, illusion,
               le tout est perdu.

L'esprit coule comme le vent.

Chevauche la brise, laisse-la t'élever,
          surprise chaque fois.
Chevauche le vent pétri de soleil
          réchauffant les lieux plus réflecteurs.

Breeze Rider

Every force of nature has a purpose.
    I maintain the planet's balance.
When people feel I'm here
    they're lifted.

Traveling through wind
    one reaches places others can't,
      a matter of quality.

The goal is to let the mind flow
    and not stagnate,
      let it rumble like a river.

If one tries to keep a little piece,
    trophy, illusion,
      the whole is lost.

The mind flows through like wind.

Ride the breeze, lift into it,
    a surprise each time.
Ride the wind drawn from sun
    heating more reflective places.

III

The way the night knows itself with the moon,
be that with me.

~ RUMI

Life's a spell so exquisite, everything conspires to break it.

~ EMILY DICKINSON

Rêveuse

Ah apercevoir Aphrodite
et être touchée par sa grâce,
voir la beauté partout,
pardonner à tous et moi-même
et succomber, succomber, succomber.

Ah donner encore une chance à l'amour
car j'ai vénéré Athéna et suivi Artémis.
Goûte la grenade de Chypre,
plonge dans l'océan,
laisse-toi briser le cœur.

Considère ceci : sois fortunée, reconnaissante,
considère ceci : sois vivante
car l'ultime cadeau est donné avec la mort.
Il n'y a ni fin ni début,
succombe, succombe, succombe.

Je paie avec la mort de ma mère
le prix de mes rêves
tandis que je rêve la création d'un monde,
tandis que je rêve de nouveaux souvenirs,
tandis que je me rêve d'amour t'inonder.

Ah laisser Aphrodite te guider vers l'esprit
suprême qui clame encore et toujours
montagnes et rivières je suis,
vent, sable et pluie je suis,
lune, soleil, étoiles je suis.

Sa voix ne sera pas étouffée
car elle est formidable
et fait écho à celles des bien aimés.
C'est son privilège de te servir
car la vie recherche beauté et complexité.

Percevras-tu avec les yeux du cœur,
entendras-tu l'appel du jaguar,
celui du colibri?
Laisse la roue du temps t'absorber,
laisse-toi briser le cœur.

Dreamer

Ah to get a glimpse of Aphrodite
and be touched by grace,
see beauty everywhere,
forgive all and myself
and surrender, surrender, surrender.

Ah to get another chance at love
for I worshipped Athena and followed Artemis.
Taste the Cyprus pomegranate,
dive into the ocean,
have your heart broken.

Consider this, be fortunate, grateful,
consider this, be alive
for the greatest gift is given with death.
There is no end and no beginning,
surrender, surrender, surrender.

I pay with my mother's death
for the price of my dreams
as I dream the world into being
as I dream new memories
as I dream myself into love falling into you.

Ah to let Aphrodite guide you to the great
spirit who proclaims again and again
mountains am I, rivers am I
wind, sand and rain am I
moon, sun and stars am I.

Her voice will not be silenced
for it is formidable
and echoes those of all beloved.
It is her privilege to serve you
for life seeks beauty and complexity.

Will you perceive with the eyes
of the heart, heed the call of jaguar
and hummingbird?
Let the wheel of time absorb you,
have your heart broken.

La quiétude de l'infini

Lors d'une visite chez mes ancêtres on m'introduit
dans le palais des hypnotiseurs
par une petite entrée et un superbe escalier circulaire,
chaque marche un tiroir contenant des sculptures.
L'étage supérieur se déploie sur d'immenses vues
offrant fontaines, centaures et autres créatures,
statues animées, étonnant spectacle.
Les fenêtres donnent sur un lac
– entouré de saules et vignes –
dont la surface lisse et argentée
reflète la beauté stupéfaite
d'âmes mouvantes le regard rivé à l'horizon.

Quiescent Infinite

On a visit to my ancestors I'm shown
into the palace of hypnotists
through a small entrance and grand rounding staircase,
each step a drawer containing sculptures.
The landing expands into huge vistas
over fountains, centaurs and other creatures,
statues come alive, stunning spectacle.
Windows open onto a lake
– adorned by willows and vines –
whose surface, smooth and silver,
reflects the astonished beauty
of mutable selves riveted on the horizon.

Un esprit comme le ciel

Plonge au cœur du troisième œil,
perle bleue, espace entre
soupirs, équilibre
total, ami et étranger.

Deviens un avec le divin,
moment alchimique. L'émotion
épouse l'intellect, esprit et ciel, bâtit
du jour au lendemain une maison du terroir,

née d'amour, de la clarté
d'être aimée à ce point,
proclame ma vérité.

Guidé par un fil invisible
deviens l'esprit
de la loi, embrasse l'ordre.

A Mind Like the Sky

Go deep into the third eye, blue
pearl, space between breaths,
place of complete equilibrium,
friend and stranger.

Become one with God,
alchemical moment. Emotion
marries intellect, mind and sky,
builds overnight a house of earth

born from love, the clarity
of being wanted
so much, claims my truth.

Guided by an invisible
thread, become the spirit
of the law, embrace the order.

Le Magicien

Bonne nuit, le soupir mélodieux
m'attrape telle une vigne,
s'enroule autour de mon désir.
Je scrute des yeux violets,
prière inexaucée,
clé de la chambre à musique.
J'échappe à mon esprit,
aspirée par la fée fleur.
Je deviens songe.

Les montagnes couronnées de neige fondent
dans les nuages, balayées par le vent
comme du sable blanchi, tableau indien hanté,
envoûtant, devin,
tous les visages là ensevelis, sculptés
vivants, en métamorphose,
insistant, *rappelle-toi qui tu es,*
sors du temps,
choisis de nourrir le loup blanc.

Couchée dans la pénombre,
submergée de musique angélique,
intoxiquée de lavande,
tout est lumière et légende.
Je sombre plus et m'élève en cercles
jusqu'à ne plus exister.

Au cœur des larmes après la pluie
l'aube se lève, des rayons
de lumière inondent mes ailes.
Brume et douleur se dissolvent.
J'ai éclaté en joie dissipant toute attente.

Étrange et inhabituelle chaque circonstance.
Le Magicien chez moi, ma structure
demeure intacte.
Je remercie tous et tout
d'être encore ici.
Le Diable est si doux, bienvenue au changement.
L'horloge déliée,
au bout de la pente sèche
cobra, loup et coyote m'acceuillent :
je renais cheval péruvien.

The Magician

Good night, the mellifluous whisper
catches me like a vine,
wraps itself around my will.
I stare at violet eyes,
unanswered prayer,
key to the music room.
I slip out of mind,
sucked into the flower fairy.
I become a dream.

The snowcapped mountains blend
into clouds, brushed by wind like whitened
sand, haunted Indian landscape,
hypnotic, soothsayer, all
the faces buried there, sculpted
alive, shape shifting, urging
me, *remember who you are,*
step outside of time,
choose to feed the white wolf.

I lie in darkness
engulfed by angels' music,
intoxicated with lavender.
All is light and legend.
I sink deeper, circle higher
until I don't exist.

Inside tears after rain,
dawn arises, rays
of light flood my wings.
Mist and pain dissolve, I burst
into joy melting down all expectations.

Strange and unusual every circumstance.
The Magician home, I know
my structure remains intact
and refuses to budge.
Thank everyone and everything I'm still here.
The Devil so sweet, I welcome change.
The clock untangled,
at the bottom of the dry slope
cobra, wolf and coyote greet me:
I'm reborn into a Peruvian horse.

Arrêt lunaire

Le désir d'atteindre
un lieu dans mon esprit
où toujours je fus bien,
me ramène
à l'innocence plaçant des roses,
certaine énigme
des années migratoires,
lune interdite.
Avec les os du crâne
j'écoute un langage de pluie,
prisme, mélodie d'un monde à venir.

Lunar Standstill

The desire to move
to a place in my mind
where I've always been well
brings me back
to innocence placing roses,
certain enigma
of migratory years,
out of bounds moon.
With the bones of the skull
I listen to a language of rain,
prism, melody of a world becoming.

La fleur la plus séduisante

Les orchidées séduisent –
cygnes sensuels à figure humaine
leurs bouches primales captivent –
cocons fantômes luisant au clair de lune
animaux subliminaux dont l'élégance
et la passion du théâtre se saturent de perfection.
Sanguines ou virginales
elles prennent quatre ans à fleurir
et jeter leur sort.
Leurs paupières iris caressent secrets de tentacules
oranges, langues pourpres, robes d'or ruisselantes
de joyaux, lèvres succulentes qui cautérisent
nos désirs immortels.
Leur audace virtuose et regards baissés
nous ensorcellent et nous convoquent à Cythère.

The Sexiest Flower

Orchids seduce –
sultry swans shaped like us
their primal mouths entice –
ghost cocoons aglow in moonlight
subliminal animals whose elegance
and passion for the theatre fixate on perfection.
Sanguine or virginal
they take four years to flower
and cast their spell.
Their iris lids caress secrets of orange
tentacles, purple tongues, gold robes dripping
jewels, luscious lips that cauterize
our desires in their everness.
Their bold mastery and downward glances
bewitch and summon us to Cythera.

Diapositives de pensées

Ouvre un livre d'images de la psyché
rempli d'animaux de bandes dessinées
qui tentent d'effrayer derrière des murs en verre.
Le tout une blague cosmique,
le défi de reconnaître mon visage dans la foule,
surprise de ne pas m'être suivie,
aveugle aux directions,
distraite par la pierre
et l'expansion de l'architecture,
soulagée de ne plus être hantée,
d'être simplement la substance du cosmos.

Transparencies of Thought

Open a picture book of psyche
filled with cartoon animals
trying to scare from behind glass walls.
The whole thing a cosmic joke,
the challenge to recognize my face
in the crowd, surprised I haven't followed
myself, blind to directions,
distracted by stone and the expansion
of architecture, relieved
to no longer be hunted,
just the substance of the cosmos.

Harmonies parallèles

Nous nous donnons la vie
en offrande, navigateurs d'océans
éphémères, marins d'ondes temporelles
subliminales, architectes de paysages
fantasques. *Accroche-toi à la crinière*, rit
le cheval qui danse, claquant
sabots au rythme des tambours.
Bousculée hors d'étroits périmètres
par l'aimant de l'univers,
forcée d'abandonner l'illusion
du puzzle qui m'habite,
je suis régie par la poésie des mathématiques,
ombre lorsque je perds forme
dans le clair-obscur de l'intuition spatiale.
Je me révèle en façonnant l'augure.
L'aigle m'enseigne
à chasser, célérité suivant
le calme, conflit chaleureux, rapace
découvrant codes secrets, principes
de combat mortel, esprit élastique.
Fascinante la passion d'une rose
pour l'eau, notre transformation en couguars
sous la pluie et celle de montagnes
immuables en nuages intangibles.
Nous mûrissons musicalement
couverts de fleurs de cerisier,
variation divine,
conscience en quête d'expansion.

Parallel Keys

We give each other an offering
  of life, voyagers on impermanent inner
    oceans, mariners on subliminal time
      waves, master builders of whimsical
landscapes. *Hold on to the mane*, the dancing
    horse laughs, clapping
      hooves in rhythm with drumbeats.
Pushed out of narrow perimeters
  by the magnet of the universe,
    forced to abandon the illusion
      of the puzzle I inhabit,
I'm governed by the poetry of mathematics,
    shadow when I lose form
      in the chiaroscuro of spatial intuition.
I reveal myself fixing the omen.
  Eagle teaches
    me to hunt, stillness followed
      by speed, warm warring, raptor
uncovering secret codes, deadly
    fighting principles, tensile mind.
Marvel at how a rose makes
  love with water, how we turn into cougars
    in the rain, how immovable mountains
      become intangible clouds.
We grow musically
  covered in cherry blossoms,
    divine variation.
We are consciousness wanting to expand.

MORE PRAISE FOR *Dreaming My Animal Selves*

To read Hélène Cardona's poems in this book is to dream the body back to a time when it still flew feathered through air, still breathed through gills, then first slumped its heft to feel sand prick its tender and virginal flesh. The French poems printed en face serve to enhance the blurring of borders in a way that is purely Cardona--as personal as a dream--but now shared.

~ DIANN BLAKELY

(author of *Farewell My Lovelies* (Academy of American Poets' Book Society's Choice)
and *Cities of Flesh and the Dead*, winner of the the Alice Fay Di Castagnola Award)

Hélène Cardona's Dreaming My Animal Selves / Le Songe de mes Âmes Animales *is a work written in English and then translated into French by the author. Cardona's antecedents are certainly exotic; born in Paris to a Greek mother and an Ibizan father, she seems at home in many languages and many countries. Well translated work takes on another life in its new language, and surely the multi-lingual author with a foot in both camps occupies a privileged position with regard to the ability to convey meaning in the most precise and appropriate idiom possible.*

The poems in this collection do concern themselves explicitly with movement, shape-shifting and liminal states of consciousness. As Cardona writes in "Dancing the Dream", "This is a story of flight, / a story of roots, / a story of grace. / I am the wandering child."

The tone of these poems is often breathless, enraptured, and to borrow a phrase once used by Charles Tomlinson brilliantly to describe the poetry of Marina Tsvetaeva, 'self-wearing'.

~ CAITRÍONA O'REILLY, *Poetry Salzburg Review*

A bilingual book, produced by one author, has a unique opportunity to play "in between" the languages, so that a third reading that falls in between the languages falls into place. In the tradition of Baudelaire who tempers a system of "correspondences" between the physical and spiritual, so Cardona transforms as she equates sound and movement into visual/auditory harmony. Even if one only reads the 23 poems, written in English, without the enhancement of the translation, the flow and musicality of the English stand on their own to create a blend of dream and myth.

~ KITTY JOSPÉ, *Poet's Talk*

Hélène Cardona has managed the impossible here: she has combined a perfect mastery of words with an exquisite imagination to explore the inner world of animals and the hidden worlds of the human heart.

The poems in DREAMING themselves have the quality of dreams, where all things are possible, and we fly

> behind a procession of swans
> to an island in the heart of Paris...
> The dream opens forgotten realms of creation.

But when I look more closely at these poems – and they are so well designed, and multi-layered, that you will also want to go back to them over and over– I was astonished by the echoes and resonances the poet has woven in her poems, and you will find winks to Ovid and Saint John Perse and H.D.

Ms. Cardona wears her erudition lightly, so that what is most evident at first is a deep sense of love for the world and a marvel of its creations: her heart has mastered possibility. I loved this book. I hope you will too. The poetry world will be talking about it for a long time.

~ MICHAEL METEYER, *Goodreads*

This book is about consciousness, too. It is about the power of place. It is about ancestral roots. It is about the strength that grows from pursing discovery. It is all about the simple beautiful experience the reader enjoys following the enchanting lyrics and their subliminal power that carry you on a voyage from the beginning of the book to the end. Finally, one of the main themes of this book simply seems to be, to me at least, the principles of pure joyfulness. And reading these poems is a truly joyous act.

~ MARK EISNER, *Poetry Flash*

These are lush, lyrically gorgeous poems written with the interior house of dreams present throughout, rich and potent metaphorical messages assimilated along the lines of possibility and depth. Cardona is a poet to watch, a singer to hear, a voice that rings with refreshing capabilities!

~ ROBERT VAUGHAN, fiction and poetry editor, *Lost in Thought*

These poems shine the most and brightest when they make a case (perhaps selfishly) for their own beauty, their strange ownness. Seduced by their own rhythm and repetition, some wild images, interesting unknowns are hatched. It is a collection of poems written with a terrific sense of music.

~ JAMES BROWNING KEPPLE, *Unlikely Blond*

One should read Hélène Cardona's Dreaming My Animal Selves *because of the refreshing treatment she gives the subjects, dreams and animals. There is the sense in Cardona's work of a reality within dreams that human beings need to tap into, in order to live fuller lives.*

It is interesting that [Mary] Oliver and Cardona take separate paths to reach the same conclusion, that of the need for the wholeness of life. This happening shows astute inventiveness on the part of Cardona. Dreamer *is one of the longer poems in the collection, and is also one of the strongest. In it Cardona lays out the benefits of living a life unhampered by conventions—a life experienced in dreams—and needs pursuit in wakefulness. The person becomes a free self in surrendering to what is experienced in dreams and living accordingly when awake. In the same poem, Cardona writes, "life needs beauty and complexity." Yes, and she wants us to embrace both. Fortunately, her work helps show the way.*

~ ELVIS ALVES, *The Compulsive Reader*

Beautifully accomplished, rendered in two languages, English and French, side by side. Vividly imagistic and mystical and inspiring the reader to a realization of a better self.

~ JENNIFER REESER
(author of *Sonnets from the Dark Lady and Other Poems*)

All the poems are soul-searching and they enchant you with their mysticism and elegance. The surrealist feel in the poems at times makes them wistful and magical. The cosmic forces of the universe, fantasy, surrealism, dreams, and many other topics are part of the theme in the poems.

~ MAMTA MADHAVAN, *Readers' Favorite*

Cardona weaves symbols of beauty, unity, and healing as her words journey through legend, myth, and magical splintered landscape. Take her hand and join with her imagination.

~ KRISTEN D. SCOTT, Editor-In-Chief *Knot Magazine*

Lovely, dreamlike poems that have the feel of A Midsummer's Night Dream *all over them.*

~ TARA L. MASIH
(author of *Where the Dog Star Never Glows*, National Best Books Award finalist)

For poetry lovers who enjoy a more whimsical and symbolic writer, then the works of French actress and poet Hélène Cardona will be right up your alley.

~ AMANDA FERRIS, *The Absolute*

In her newest book, Dreaming My Animal Selves, *imparted in both English and French, poet and actress Hélène Cardona opens for humanity a vision of our place within creation, our deepest memory, and the divine mystery that surrounds us at all times... In reading these poems I am reminded of something a friend once told me. That each artist must form a new language in every work of art they create.*

With a master artist's hand, she helps us to see beyond our normal everyday vision into an astonishing world that is surrounded by beauty and light... Her words reclaim for us the perfect sight found within our own imaginations and spiritual being, the human psyche.

.... a divine eternal dance, a perichoresis, an indwelling of the divine spirit actively at work within the world, in a world without end. Dreaming My Animal Selves *captures this feeling, this divine dance in a wonderful choreography of words and images.*

~ RON STARBUCK, *Saint Julian Press*

I thoroughly enjoyed reading Hélène's poems in French and English, the wee quotes and dedications gave a delightful personal touch too. But of course it is her imagination, the scenes she sets and her weaving of nature with magic that truly captivate the reader.

~ ELISHA GABRIEL, *The Absurd Word Bird*

A citizen of the U.S., France & Spain, HÉLÈNE CARDONA is a poet, linguist, translator & actor. She taught at Hamilton College & Loyola Marymount University, translated for the Canadian Embassy & NEA, received a Master's in American Literature from the Sorbonne and fellowships from the Goethe-Institut & the Universidad Internacional de Andalucía.

She is author of *The Astonished Universe*, is notably published in *Washington Square*, *World Literature Today*, *The Warwick Review*, *Poetry Salzburg Review*, *Dublin Review of Books*, *Recours au Poème*, *The Irish Literary Times*, *Periódico de Poesía*, & *Poetry International*, and is co-editor of *Dublin Poetry Review*, *Levure Littéraire*, and *Fulcrum*. She was guest speaker at Brown University & The Puterbaugh International Literary Festival at Oklahoma State University.

Acting credits include *Chocolat*, *Dawn of the Planet of the Apes*, *X-Men: Days of Future Past*, *The Hundred-Foot Journey*, *Mumford*, *Happy Feet 2*, *Muppets Most Wanted*, etc. For *Serendipity* she co-wrote with director Peter Chelsom & composer Alan Silvestri the song *Lucienne*, which she also sang.